Also by MARVEN BILLS

The Principles Governing Wealth & Finance

The Principles Governing Wealth & Finance

MARVEN BILLS

Published by MARVEN BILLS, 2024.

THE PRINCIPLES GOVERNING WEALTH & FINANCE

First edition. February 4, 2024.

ISBN: 979-8223007234

Written by MARVEN BILLS.

Table of Contents

This book is dedicated to Mr. Jeremiah Tengan.

THE
PRINCIPLES GOVERNING WEALTH
&
FINANCE

Mastering The Global Wealth Ethics

Marven Bills

INTRODUCTION

What if, instead of guessing, you could get the inside scoop from those who had really amassed wealth? Imagine if you could learn the strategies used by the wealthiest people and companies in the world to achieve unprecedented levels of success in the financial sector. What if you could use this information to reach your career and personal objectives, and finally get the financial independence you've always wanted?

This book will provide you with the answers you're seeking to these issues. In this book, you will understand the principles controlling wealth and finance, based on the knowledge and experience of some of the most powerful and renowned experts in the industry. Whether you are a student, an entrepreneur, an employee, a novice, or a retiree, you will also discover how to apply these principles to your personal life.

Do not expect a magic bullet or a fast fix from this book. The fundamentals of wealth development and management are covered in this thorough and useful reference, which includes:

- Creating objectives and a strategy
- Saving money and getting a better education
- Keeping track of money and debt

Making smart financial decisions, including: - Saving and investing - Keeping your assets and income safe - Comprehending how taxes and inflation affect your finances - Establishing and maintaining a solid credit history - Harnessing the power of compound interest and diversification - Steering clear of typical scams and pitfalls - Adjusting to new opportunities and changes in the market

By following the concepts and techniques presented in this book, you will be able to:

- Increase your income and net worth - Reduce your financial stress and risk - Enhance your financial knowledge and confidence - Achieve your short-term and long-term objectives
- Support your family and community
- Make a good effect on the world

This book is not simply about money. It is about building a full and meaningful life, based on your beliefs and vision. It is about identifying your purpose and passion, and utilizing your riches as a vehicle to achieve them. It is about living a life of plenty and thankfulness, and sharing your talents and benefits with others.

Whether you are seeking for a means to better your financial condition, or you are already on the route to riches and success, this book will give you with essential insights and ideas that will help you realize your full potential. This book will teach you that wealth and money are not just ruled by numbers and formulae, but also by ideas and practices that anybody can learn and use.

Are you ready to take command of your financial destiny? Are you ready to master the mysteries of money and finance? Are you ready to alter your life and the lives of people around you?

If so, then this book is for you. Welcome to the universe of rules controlling wealth and money.

Chapter 1

The Foundations of Wealth and Finance

Money and wealth are major ideas that have far-reaching consequences for every one of us. Wealth is the total worth of all the assets that a person or a group holds, such as money, property, stocks, bonds, etc. Investing, saving, borrowing, and spending are all parts of managing money, and the study of these topics is known as finance.

Wealth and finance are connected, but not the same. Wealth refers to an individual's material possessions, whereas finance refers to the means by which such possessions may be put to use in pursuit of certain objectives. As an example, even if someone is very wealthy, they risk losing or wasting it all if they aren't careful with their spending. Contrarily, one may make do with very little money and still grow it or even produce more value if they are strategic with their spending.

One of the major purposes of finance is to produce more money, or to improve the value of the present riches. Putting money into enterprises, initiatives, or assets with the potential to provide income or capital appreciation is one way to achieve this goal. Saving money or minimizing the likelihood of losing it is another objective of financial planning. A diversified portfolio or the use of insurance or derivatives to hedge against loss are two ways to achieve this goal.

There are a lot of things that might affect one's financial condition and wealth: the economy, politics, social mores, the law, technical advancements, individual tastes, moral principles, etc. These variables impact the supply and demand of wealth, the cost and availability of financing, the possibilities and problems of wealth production and protection, and the distribution and redistribution of wealth across various groups and people.

The effects of money and wealth on both individuals and society are substantial. On the one hand, wealth and finance may facilitate economic progress, social development, and human well-being, by providing the means and incentives for production, consumption, and innovation. On the other side, wealth and finance may also produce economic instability, social inequity, and human misery, by causing the issues and conflicts of scarcity, inefficiency, and injustice.

Therefore, wealth and money are not merely questions of numbers and formulas, but also matters of values and decisions. How we comprehend, manage, and apply our money and cash reflects our vision, mission, and purpose in life. Wealth and finance may be instruments for good or evil, depending on how we utilize them and for what objectives. As such, wealth and money need not just knowledge and abilities, but also judgment and ethics.

What is Wealth and Why Does It Matter?

Wealth is a phrase that may have varied connotations for different individuals. Some may describe wealth as possessing a lot of money, assets, or things. Others may describe wealth as having excellent health, enjoyment, or relationships. Some may even describe riches as having a feeling of purpose, satisfaction, or meaning in life.

However, no matter how we define wealth, it is evident that wealth counts. Wealth may influence several elements of our life, such as our well-being, opportunities, choices, and impact. In this article, I will discuss some of the reasons why money matters, and how we might obtain and utilize riches in a constructive manner.

First, money matters because it may alter our well-being. Well-being is the condition of being comfortable, healthy, or cheerful. Wealth may contribute to our well-being by providing us with the essential requirements of life, such as food, water, shelter, clothes, and health care. Without these demands, humans may suffer from hunger, thirst, exposure, illness, or death. Wealth may also boost our well-being by enabling us to enjoy the better things in life, such as education, entertainment, travel, or hobbies. These things may enhance our brains, bodies, and souls, and make us feel happier and more fulfilled.

However, riches may also hurt our well-being if we abuse it or grow obsessed with it. Wealth may drive us to greed, jealousy, pride, or arrogance, which can ruin our relationships, morality, or principles. Wealth may also drive us to stress, worry, or dread, which can impair our mental, emotional, or physical health. Wealth may also distract us from the things that actually important in life, such as love, generosity, or appreciation, which can make us feel empty or dissatisfied.

Therefore, money counts for our well-being, but we need to utilize it carefully and sparingly, and not allow it rule us or define us.

Second, money matters because it may alter our prospects. Opportunities are the chances or possibilities that we have to accomplish something or achieve something. Wealth may generate or increase our prospects by providing us access to additional resources, knowledge, or networks. For example, riches may enable us seek further education, establish a company, or tour the globe. Wealth may also help us overcome or avoid some of the hurdles or problems that we may encounter, such as poverty, prejudice, or violence. Wealth may also assist us support or empower people who have fewer chances, such as our family, friends, or community.

However, it may also restrict or diminish our chances if we abuse it or get comfortable with it. Wealth may make us sluggish, selfish, or wasteful, which can impede us from learning, developing, or improving. Wealth may also make us uneducated, insensitive, or uncaring, which can prohibit us from understanding, empathizing, or assisting others. Wealth may also make us arrogant, entitled, or disrespectful, which might prohibit us from appreciating, respecting, or partnering with others.

Therefore, money counts for our chances, but we need to utilize it carefully and generously, and not allow it separate us or alienate us.

Third, money matters because it may alter our decisions. Choices are the choices or acts that we make or take in our life. Wealth may affect or mold our decisions by providing us greater alternatives, freedom, or power. For example, money may assist us pick where to live, what to do, or who to be. Wealth may also assist us determine how to spend our time, money, or energy. Wealth may also assist us determine what to value, believe, or support.

However, riches may also confine or distort our choices if we abuse it or grow addicted to it. Wealth may make us greedy, egotistical, or dishonest, which can drive us to make unwise or dangerous decisions. Wealth may also make us blind, stupid, or reckless, which might drive us to make unreasonable or unsafe decisions. Wealth may also make us reliant, insecure, or unhappy, which might cause us to make unsatisfactory or regretful decisions.

Therefore, money counts for our decisions, but we need to utilize it carefully and intelligently, and not allow it corrupt us or fool us.

Finally, money matters because it may change our effect. Impact is the impact or influence that we have on ourselves, others, or the world. Wealth may expand or improve our effect by providing us additional resources, talents, or reach. For example, riches may enable us invent or innovate something that can benefit ourselves, others, or the globe. Wealth may also enable us contribute or donate something that can assist or inspire ourselves, others, or the planet. Wealth may also help us modify or enhance anything that can solve or avoid a problem for ourselves, others, or the globe.

However, riches may also lessen or exacerbate our effect if we abuse it or grow apathetic to it. Wealth may make us destructive, dangerous, or wasteful, which can injure or destroy ourselves, others, or the planet. Wealth may also make us indifferent, apathetic, or cynical, which might overlook or neglect oneself, others, or the planet. Wealth may also make us arrogant, egotistical, or greedy, which can exploit or oppress ourselves, others, or the globe.

Therefore, money counts for our effect, but we need to utilize it constructively and responsibly, and not allow it harm ourselves or the planet.

In conclusion, wealth is a phrase that might have diverse connotations for different individuals, yet it is apparent that it counts. Wealth may influence several elements of our life, such as our well-being, opportunities, choices, and impact. Wealth may be a gift or a punishment, depending on how we utilize it or connect to it. Wealth may make us happy or miserable, free or chained, strong or weak, good or evil. Wealth may make ourselves better or worse, and the world better or worse. Therefore, we need to be conscious, thoughtful, and purposeful about our riches, and utilize it in a manner that may benefit ourselves, others, and the planet.

The Role of Finance in Wealth Creation and Distribution

Finance is the study and practice of managing money and other assets. It includes numerous actions such as saving, investing, borrowing, lending, budgeting, and allocating resources. Finance plays a significant role in wealth generation and distribution, since it helps people, corporations, and governments to fulfill their economic objectives and enhance their living standards.

Wealth creation is the process of increasing the value of assets or income over time. Finance helps wealth generation by offering opportunities and instruments for saving and investing. Saving is the act of laying away a part of money for future consumption. Investing is the act of utilizing money to acquire assets that create returns or grow in value. Both saving and investing help people and corporations acquire money and prepare for future needs and possibilities.

Finance also aids wealth growth by offering access to credit and capital markets. Credit is the capacity to borrow money and return it later with interest. Capital markets are the venues where financial securities, such as stocks and bonds, are issued and exchanged. Credit and capital markets offer funding for people and enterprises to start, develop, or upgrade their activities. They also help investors to diversify their investments and lower their risks. By enabling the movement of capital and information, finance supports economic development and innovation.

Wealth distribution is the manner that wealth is shared or distributed among various groups or people in a community. Finance impacts wealth distribution by changing the rewards and hazards of various assets and activities. Finance also influences the rules and organizations that regulate how wealth is taxed, transferred, or redistributed. For example, finance may alter the amount and structure of taxes, which affects how much income the government gets and how it spends it. Finance may also impact the design and execution of social programs, such as welfare, education, health care, and pensions, which affect the well-being and opportunities of diverse groups of the population.

Finance may have both beneficial and bad consequences on wealth distribution, depending on how it is utilized and governed. On the one hand, finance may increase wealth distribution by boosting financial inclusion and knowledge. Financial inclusion is the availability and usage of relevant and affordable financial services by all people and companies. Financial literacy is the knowledge and abilities to make informed and successful financial choices. Both financial inclusion and literacy may enable individuals to engage in the economy and enhance their financial fortunes. On the other side, finance may exacerbate wealth distribution by producing or aggravating financial inequality and instability. Financial inequality is the unequal distribution of wealth or income among various groups or people. Financial instability is the occurrence of substantial and unanticipated changes in financial markets or institutions. Both financial disparity and volatility may hinder social cohesiveness and economic progress.

In conclusion, finance plays a significant role in wealth creation and distribution, as it influences the allocation and management of resources in the economy and society. Finance may assist people, corporations, and governments to enhance their wealth and improve their living conditions. However, finance may also produce or intensify issues like as financial inequality and instability, which can impair the well-being and possibilities of diverse groups or people. Therefore, money should be utilized and controlled in a responsible and sustainable way, with the purpose of establishing a fair and efficient distribution of wealth.

Chapter 2

Principles Of Building Wealth

WEALTH IS THE NUMBER of valuable resources or assets that one owns. It may be quantified in numerous ways, such as income, net worth, or level of life. Building wealth is the act of growing one's wealth over time, via numerous ways such as saving, investing, earning, or producing value. Building money may have various advantages, such as financial stability, independence, enjoyment, and societal effect. However, accumulating money is not simple, and it involves following basic principles that might guide one's choices and activities. Here are some of the fundamentals of creating wealth:

Spend less than you earn

The most fundamental premise of generating money is to spend less than you make. This suggests that one should have a positive cash flow, where the revenue surpasses the costs. This helps one to conserve money and avoid debt, which may destroy one's wealth. Spending less than you make also demands maintaining a budget, where one records and regulates one's income and spending, and sets reasonable and attainable objectives. Spending less than you make also denotes living within or below one's means, where one avoids needless or lavish spending, and prioritizes one's necessities above one's desires.

Invest intelligently

Another key of creating money is to invest intelligently. This suggests that one should utilize one's savings to produce additional income or value, by placing them into productive assets, such as stocks, bonds, real estate, or enterprises. Investing intelligently also demands having a long-term perspective, where one concentrates on the development and compounding of one's wealth, rather than the short-term swings or returns. Investing properly also implies diversifying one's portfolio, where one distributes one's risk across multiple kinds of assets, industries, or markets, and avoids placing all one's eggs in one basket. Investing properly also implies being informed and educated, where one learns and investigates about the different investing possibilities, techniques, and dangers, and seeks professional or expert guidance when required.

Earn more

Another key of gaining wealth is to earn more. This suggests that one should enhance one's income, by developing one's abilities, knowledge, or credentials, and finding better or more possibilities in one's work or company. Earning more also demands having a growth mentality, where one accepts difficulties, learns from setbacks, and seeks criticism and progress. Earning more also involves being proactive and innovative, where one takes initiative, solves issues, and generates value for others. Earning more also involves being adaptive and flexible, where one adapts to changes, trends, or needs in the market or society, and exploits one's talents or hobbies.

Create value

Another concept of developing wealth is to produce value. This suggests that one should contribute to the well-being or enjoyment of others, by giving products, services, or solutions that suit their needs, wants, or desires. Creating value also needs having a vision or purpose, where one has a clear and compelling understanding of what one wants to do or provide to the world. Creating value also involves being unique and original, where one produces new or better methods of doing things, and stands out from the crowd. Creating value also involves being generous and ethical, where one shares one's riches, knowledge, or talents with others, and behaves with integrity and responsibility.

Building money is a worthy and satisfying objective, but it is neither easy or straightforward. It demands following basic principles that might help one make wise and successful judgments and activities. These principles are: spend less than you earn, invest wisely, earn more, and generate value. By implementing these ideas, one may enhance one's wealth over time, and enjoy the advantages of financial stability, independence, enjoyment, and social influence.

Setting Goals and Developing a Plan

Goals are the desirable results that one wishes to attain in life, career, or any other sphere. Goals might be short-term or long-term, particular or generic, personal or professional, and so on. Setting objectives is crucial since it enables one to define one's vision, concentrate one's efforts, assess one's progress, and inspire oneself to overcome problems.

However, creating objectives is not enough. One also has to establish a strategy to reach those aims. A plan is a sequence of activities or actions that one plans to follow to attain one's objectives. A plan might be precise or flexible, depending on the nature and complexity of the aims. Developing a plan is crucial since it enables one to organize one's resources, prioritize one's duties, predict possible issues, and measure one's performance.

There are various approaches and tools that might allow one to create objectives and construct a strategy. One of the most famous and successful ones is the SMART framework. SMART stands for Specific, Measurable, Achievable, Relevant, and Time-bound. According to this paradigm, a good aim should contain the following characteristics:

- Specific: The purpose should be obvious and well-defined, not unclear or confusing. For example, instead of expressing "I want to be healthy", one should state "I want to lose 10 kg in 6 months".

- Measurable: The aim should be measurable and verifiable, not subjective or abstract. For example, instead of expressing "I want to improve my skills", one should say "I want to complete an online course in Python programming".

- Achievable: The aim should be practical and achievable, not unattainable or absurd. For example, instead of expressing "I want to be a millionaire", one could say "I want to save $10,000 in a year".

- Relevant: The aim should be connected with one's values and interests, not irrelevant or contradicting. For example, instead of expressing "I want to learn French", one should add "I want to learn French because I love the culture and I want to travel to Paris".

- Time-bound: The aim should have a deadline or a timetable, not indefinite or open-ended. For example, instead of expressing "I want to read more books", one could say "I want to read one book per week for the next three months".

Once one has identified SMART objectives, one may proceed to build a strategy to attain them. A good plan should contain the following elements:

- Tasks: The plan should break down the objective into smaller and doable tasks or sub-goals. For example, if the aim is to lose 10 kg in 6 months, the tasks may be to exercise for 30 minutes every day, to eat a balanced diet, and to drink enough of water.

- Resources: The plan should indicate the resources that one needs to fulfill the objectives or sub-goals. Resources might be material, human, or informational. For example, if the job is to exercise for 30 minutes every day, the resources may be a gym membership, a fitness trainer, or a workout app.

- Schedule: The plan should provide a schedule or a frequency to each job or sub-goal. The timetable should be realistic and adaptable, taking into consideration one's availability, preferences, and limits. For example, if the aim is to eat a balanced diet, the timetable may be to develop a weekly meal plan, to buy for goods on Sundays, and to cook at home on weekdays.

- Evaluation: The plan should contain a mechanism to monitor and assess one's progress and performance. Evaluation may be done by employing indicators, feedback, or self-reflection. For example, if the aim is to finish an online course in Python programming, the assessment may be to take quizzes, to submit assignments, or to analyze one's learning results.

In conclusion, defining objectives and making a plan are crucial abilities for anybody who wishes to attain success and fulfillment in life, business, or any other arena. By applying the SMART framework and the characteristics of a successful plan, one may create clear, realistic, and meaningful objectives, and develop effective, structured, and adaptive strategies to attain them.

Investing in Education and Skills

Education and skills are crucial for the growth of people, society, and economies. Education equips individuals with the information, values, and competences that allow them to engage in social, cultural, and political life. Skills are the talents and capabilities that individuals gain through learning and practice, which enable them to accomplish tasks and solve issues in many circumstances. Investing in education and skills involves dedicating money, time, and effort to increase the quality, accessibility, and relevance of learning opportunities for everyone.

Investing in education and skills has numerous advantages for people and society. For people, education and skills may boost their human capital, which is the store of knowledge, skills, and talents that they possess and can utilize to produce income and well-being. Human capital may boost people's productivity, employability, and incomes, as well as their health, happiness, and civic involvement. For society, education and skills may create social cohesion, cultural diversity, and democratic principles, as well as economic prosperity, innovation, and competitiveness. Education and skills may also help to alleviating poverty, inequality, and social isolation, as well as tackling global concerns such as climate change, migration, and pandemics.

Investing in education and skills demands a holistic and lifelong strategy, which emphasizes the variety of learners and learning paths, and the interconnectedness of various levels and kinds of education and skills. Investing in education and skills should include the following dimensions:

- Early childhood education and care, which establishes the framework for cognitive, social, and emotional development, and prepares children for formal schooling and lifetime learning.

- Basic education, which guarantees that all children and youth learn the necessary reading, numeracy, and life skills, and have access to quality and inclusive education that respects their rights, needs, and potentials.

- Secondary and tertiary education, which improves and enhances the knowledge and skills of young people and adults, and prepares them for further education, vocational training, or the job market.

- Technical and vocational education and training, which educates individuals with the specialized skills and competences that are sought by businesses and industries, and boosts their employability and career prospects.

- Adult education and learning, which allows individuals to update and improve their skills and abilities throughout their lifetimes, and to adapt to changing social and economic situations.

- Non-formal and informal learning, which acknowledges and appreciates the learning that takes place outside the traditional education system, such as in the family, community, business, or online.

Investing in education and skills is not just a moral obligation, but also a wise investment. According to the World Bank, each extra year of schooling boosts an individual's wages by 10%, and each additional dollar spent in education provides 10 to 15 dollars in economic growth. Moreover, investment in education and skills may have good spillover effects on other areas, such as health, environment, and security. Therefore, investing in education and skills is vital for reaching the Sustainable Development Goals, which are a set of global aims for eliminating poverty, safeguarding the planet, and guaranteeing peace and prosperity for everyone by 2030.

To conclusion, investing in education and skills is one of the most effective methods to enhance the lives of people and the well-being of society. Education and skills are the main drivers of human development, societal advancement, and economic success. Investing in education and skills needs a comprehensive and coordinated plan, which includes the involvement of governments, educators, employers, civic society, and learners. Investing in education and skills is not only a duty, but also an opportunity, for building a better future for ourselves and the generations to come.

Chapter 3

Principles of Managing Wealth

WEALTH IS THE AMOUNT of valuable resources or assets that one owns. It may include money, property, investments, companies, or other types of capital. Managing money is the act of utilizing, maintaining, and expanding one's wealth in a manner that matches with one's objectives, values, and needs. Managing money may be tough, since it includes making complicated choices, balancing risks and benefits, and coping with uncertainties and changes. However, by following certain fundamental rules, one may enhance their financial well-being and attain their intended objectives. Here are some of the principles of managing wealth:

1. Know your net wealth

The first step in managing wealth is to identify your net worth, which is the difference between your assets and liabilities. Your assets are the items that you possess, such as cash, bank accounts, stocks, bonds, real estate, or personal belongings. Your obligations are the items that you owe, such as loans, mortgages, credit cards, or taxes. To determine your net worth, you need to add up the value of all your assets and minus the value of all your obligations. This will offer you a clear view of your financial condition and help you create realistic objectives and priorities.

2. Spend less than you earn

The second concept of managing wealth is to spend less than you make, which indicates that you should have a positive cash flow. Cash flow is the amount of money that you get and spend in a specific period of time, such as a month or a year. Having a positive cash flow indicates that you have more money coming in than going out, which enables you to save, invest, or pay off debt. To attain a positive cash flow, you need to design and implement a budget, which is a plan that details your income and spending. A budget may help you manage your spending patterns, find areas where you can decrease expenditures, and allocate your money to your needs and goals.

3. Save and invest intelligently

The third element of managing wealth is to save and invest intelligently, which implies that you should put your money to work for you. Saving and investing may help you expand your wealth over time, since your money might produce interest, dividends, or capital gains. Saving and investing may also help you prepare for crises, retirement, or other long-term objectives. To save and invest successfully, you need to have a defined aim, a time horizon, and a risk tolerance. A purpose is the reason why you are saving or investing, such as purchasing a home, establishing a company, or touring the globe. A time horizon is the period of time that you expect to save or invest, such as short-term, medium-term, or long-term. A risk tolerance is the degree of uncertainty that you are ready to take, such as low, moderate, or high. Based on these variables, you may pick the proper saving or investment vehicles, such as savings accounts, certificates of deposit, bonds, equities, mutual funds, or exchange-traded funds.

4. Diversify your portfolio

The fourth concept of managing wealth is to diversify your portfolio, which indicates that you should distribute your money among various sorts of assets, industries, markets, or geographies. Diversification may help you lower your risk, since it can prevent you from losing all your money if one asset, industry, market, or area performs badly. Diversification may also help you enhance your returns, since it can expose you to additional chances and development prospects. To diversify your portfolio, you need to assess your objectives, time horizon, and risk tolerance, and pick a mix of assets that meets your profile. You also need to check and rebalance your portfolio frequently, to ensure that it stays aligned with your aims and tastes.

5. Seek professional counsel

The fifth guideline of managing money is to seek professional counsel, which implies that you should speak with specialists who can help you with your financial choices. Professional counsel may help you obtain additional information, ideas, and views, as well as prevent typical errors and problems. Professional counsel may also help you save time, money, and worry, as well as obtain better results and outcomes. To seek professional guidance, you need to identify a skilled, trustworthy, and experienced financial planner, adviser, or manager, who can understand your circumstances, objectives, and requirements, and offer you with unique and complete answers. You also need to contact and interact with your adviser often, to ensure that you are on the same page and that your strategy is operating properly.

Managing money is a critical skill that may boost one's quality of life and happiness. By following the principles of managing wealth, such as knowing your net worth, spending less than you earn, saving and investing wisely, diversifying your portfolio, and seeking professional advice, one can achieve financial success and security, as well as fulfill their personal and professional aspirations. Managing money is not a one-time event, but a continual and dynamic process that involves ongoing learning, adaptation, and progress. Therefore, one should constantly endeavor to improve their financial literacy, abilities, and habits, and seek new chances and challenges that might help them develop their wealth and accomplish their objectives.

Managing Debt and Spending

Debt and spending are two crucial areas of personal finance that may have a big influence on one's financial well-being. Debt is the amount of money that one owes to others, such as banks, credit card companies, or people. Spending is the amount of money that one spends to acquire things and services, such as food, clothes, entertainment, or education. Both debt and expenditure may be useful or destructive, depending on how they are handled.

Benefits and Risks of Debt and Spending

Debt may be helpful when it is utilized to invest in one's future, such as by taking a student loan to seek higher education, or by getting a mortgage to purchase a house. Debt may also allow one to overcome temporary financial challenges, such as by using a credit card to pay for an unexpected medical payment or automobile repair. However, debt may also be destructive when it is used to support unneeded or excessive expenditure, such as by purchasing luxury products or gambling. Debt may also become a hardship when it accumulates beyond one's capacity to repay, resulting to excessive interest rates, late fees, penalties, or even bankruptcy.

Spending may be good when it is utilized to address one's fundamental requirements, such as by purchasing healthy food, comfortable clothes, or secure housing. Spending may also boost one's quality of life, such as by purchasing educational resources, leisure activities, or charity gifts. However, spending may also be destructive when it surpasses one's income, leading to debt, savings depletion, or financial instability. Spending may also become a problem when it is motivated by impulse, emotion, or social pressure, rather than by sensible planning and budgeting.

Strategies for Managing Debt and Spending

To manage debt and spending efficiently, one has to adopt specific measures that may assist to balance one's income and costs, and to reach one's financial objectives. Some of these tactics are:

• Track your income and expenses: One should maintain a record of how much money one makes and spends each month, and classify the spending into necessary and discretionary. This may assist to discover the causes and trends of one's debt and expenditure, and to locate areas where one can save or cut expenses.

• Make a budget and adhere to it: One should determine how much money one can afford to spend on various categories of costs each month, and designate some money for savings and debt payback. One should also check one's expenditure and compare it with the budget, and make modifications as appropriate. One should avoid spending more than one's income, and avoid utilizing debt to support expenditure that is not in the budget.

• Prioritize your debt repayment: One should pay off the loan that has the highest interest rate or the lowest amount first, and make more than the minimum payment if feasible. One should also avoid taking on additional debt or utilizing debt to pay off previous debt, unless it is part of a consolidation or refinancing strategy. One should also seek professional aid or therapy if one is battling with debt or facing legal action from creditors.

• Set realistic and precise financial goals: One should have a clear vision of what one wants to do with one's money, such as saving for retirement, purchasing a vehicle, or touring the globe. One should also define a schedule and a target amount for each objective, and break it down into smaller and doable stages. One should also evaluate and revise one's objectives often, and celebrate one's progress and triumphs.

• Develop good spending habits: One should spend money sensibly and thoughtfully, rather than impulsively and emotionally. One should also discriminate between one's necessities and desires, and avoid purchasing goods that one does not need or cannot afford. One should also evaluate costs and quality before purchasing, and seek for discounts, coupons, or deals. One should also minimize one's exposure to advertising, peer pressure, or social media that might impact one's purchasing choices.

Conclusion

Managing debt and spending is an important skill that may allow one to better one's financial status and well-being. By adopting certain easy and successful tactics, one may lower one's debt, improve one's savings, and attain one's financial objectives. One may also enjoy the advantages of debt and spending, without suffering from the dangers and troubles. Managing debt and spending is not simply an issue of money, but also a matter of thinking and conduct.

Saving and Investing

SAVING AND INVESTING are two essential elements of personal finance that may help people reach their financial objectives and ensure their future. Saving refers to saving away a part of one's income for future use, whereas investing refers to spending one's money to acquire assets that may create income or grow in value over time. Both saving and investing have advantages and downsides, and the appropriate balance between them relies on several aspects such as one's income, spending, risk tolerance, time horizon, and financial ambitions.

One of the key advantages of saving is that it gives liquidity, which implies that one may access their money readily and fast when required. Saving may also help one manage with unanticipated events, such as medical expenses, auto repairs, or job loss, without having to borrow money or sell their possessions. Saving may also help one prepare for short-term or medium-term objectives, such as purchasing a vehicle, a home, or a trip. Saving may help alleviate tension and anxiety, since one does not have to worry about running out of money or living paycheck to paycheck.

However, saving also has significant negatives, such as poor returns, inflation risk, and opportunity cost. Saving frequently delivers minimal returns, since the interest rates on savings accounts, certificates of deposit, or money market funds are often lower than the inflation rate, which implies that the buying value of one's money falls with time. Inflation risk refers to the chance that the costs of goods and services grow faster than the interest rate on one's savings, which diminishes the actual worth of one's money. Opportunity cost refers to the potential income or growth that one might have received by investing their money in other assets, such as stocks, bonds, or real estate, instead of conserving it.

Investing, on the other hand, has the potential to give better returns, beat inflation, and create wealth over time. Investing entails purchasing assets that may create income, such as dividends, interest, or rent, or grow in value, such as capital gains or equity. Investing may help one attain long-term objectives, such as retirement, education, or company development. Investing may also give diversification, which implies that one can spread their money over multiple sorts of assets, such as stocks, bonds, commodities, or currencies, to minimize their risk and boost their profits.

However, investing also has significant negatives, like as volatility, risk, and costs. Volatility refers to the variations in the pricing of assets, which may cause one's portfolio to increase or decline in value over time. Risk refers to the chance of losing part or all of one's money owing to market downturns, economic recessions, or unwise investment selections. Fees relate to the costs that one needs to pay to acquire, sell, or manage their assets, such as brokerage commissions, mutual fund expenditures, or financial adviser fees.

Therefore, saving and investing are both crucial for personal money, but they have distinct benefits and downsides. The best balance between saving and investing relies on one's specific position and preferences. Generally, one should save enough money to pay their basic living costs, emergency fund, and short-term or medium-term objectives, and invest the balance of their money to accomplish their long-term goals and expand their wealth. One should also evaluate their risk tolerance, time horizon, and financial ambitions while picking the suitable saving and investing techniques and products. By saving and investing intelligently, one may enhance their financial well-being and fulfill their ambitions.

Chapter 4

Principles of Protecting Wealth

WEALTH IS THE COLLECTION of valuable assets that may offer income, security, and opportunity for oneself and one's family. However, wealth is not static; it may rise or fall based on different variables such as inflation, taxes, market movements, spending patterns, and unanticipated occurrences. Therefore, it is necessary to safeguard one's money against erosion and loss, and to expand it over time. In this post, I will cover some of the fundamentals of safeguarding wealth, such as diversification, risk management, tax preparation, and estate planning.

Diversification

One of the basic concepts of safeguarding wealth is diversification, which implies spreading one's assets over numerous asset classes, industries, countries, and techniques. Diversification decreases the exposure to any one source of risk, and enables one to profit from the success of multiple markets and businesses. For example, if one invests primarily in equities, they may risk huge losses during a market collapse or a recession. However, if they also invest in bonds, real estate, commodities, and other assets, they may be able to offset some of the losses and keep their wealth. Diversification also helps to capture the potential returns from multiple sources of development and innovation, such as new markets, technology, and biotechnology.

Risk Management

Another element of preserving wealth is risk management, which entails recognizing, quantifying, and limiting the potential losses that may come from different sources of uncertainty. Risk management entails measuring one's risk tolerance, risk capacity, and risk exposure, and altering one's portfolio appropriately. Risk tolerance is the degree of volatility and loss that one is willing and able to bear in pursuit of better returns. Risk capacity is the amount of risk that one can afford to incur without endangering their financial objectives and responsibilities. Risk exposure is the real degree of risk that one is incurring in their portfolio, depending on the features and correlations of their assets. Risk management helps to match one's portfolio with their aims and limits, and to prevent taking unneeded or excessive risks that may imperil their wealth.

Tax Planning

A third aspect of conserving wealth is tax planning, which includes reducing the amount of taxes that one has to pay on their income, capital gains, dividends, interest, and inheritance. Tax planning entails comprehending the tax rules and regulations that relate to one's position, and taking advantage of the available deductions, credits, exemptions, and deferrals. Tax planning also entails picking the right tax structures and vehicles for one's assets, such as retirement accounts, trusts, foundations, and offshore organizations. Tax planning helps to lower the tax burden and raise the net return on one's wealth.

Estate Planning

A fourth aspect of conserving money is estate planning, which includes arranging for the transfer of one's fortune to their heirs and beneficiaries after their death. Estate planning entails writing a will, a trust, or a mix of both, that defines how one's assets will be dispersed, who will administer them, and who will inherit them. Estate planning also entails naming the guardians, executors, trustees, and beneficiaries, and ensuring that they are aware of and agree with one's desires. Estate planning helps to prevent probate, decrease estate taxes, safeguard one's assets from creditors and litigation, and guarantee that one's legacy is maintained and recognized.

Conclusion

Protecting money is an important and continuing activity that involves careful planning, monitoring, and modification. By adopting the concepts of diversification, risk management, tax planning, and estate planning, one may secure their money from numerous risks and uncertainties, and boost their financial well-being and security. Protecting money is not just a question of personal interest, but also a matter of social obligation, since it allows one to contribute to the welfare of their family, community, and society.

Protecting Your Assets and Income

Your assets and income are the cornerstone of your financial stability and well-being. They enable you to satisfy your fundamental necessities, attain your ambitions, and enjoy your life. However, your assets and income might also be exposed to numerous dangers, including as theft, fraud, litigation, natural catastrophes, accidents, sickness, incapacity, or death. Therefore, it is necessary to take precautions to safeguard your assets and income from these possible hazards.

One of the most effective methods to safeguard your possessions and income is to have proper insurance coverage. Insurance is a contract between you and an insurance company, where you pay a premium in return for the business's guarantee to pay for specific losses or damages that may occur. Insurance may assist you cover the costs of repairing or rebuilding your property, paying for medical expenditures, providing income replacement, or compensating for legal responsibilities. There are several sorts of insurance, such as house, vehicle, health, life, disability, liability, and umbrella insurance. You should assess your insurance requirements and possibilities often, and pick the products that fit your position and budget.

Another method to preserve your assets and income is to establish a varied investment portfolio. Investing is the act of putting your money to work in order to gain more money over time. Investing may help you develop your wealth, accomplish your financial objectives, and fight inflation. However, investing also carries dangers, such as market volatility, interest rate changes, inflation, or loss of investment. Therefore, it is vital to diversify your assets, which includes distributing your money across several asset classes, such as stocks, bonds, cash, real estate, or commodities. Diversification may help you limit your exposure to any particular risk factor, and raise your chances of achieving good returns over the long run.

A third strategy to preserve your assets and income is to develop a complete estate plan. Estate planning is the process of preparing for the management and distribution of your assets and income after your death. Estate planning may help you guarantee that your desires are followed, your loved ones are taken care of, your taxes are reduced, and your legacy is protected. Estate planning requires various procedures, such as writing a will, forming a trust, identifying beneficiaries, assigning executors, guardians, and trustees, and preparing advance directives. You should contact a trained expert, such as a lawyer, an accountant, or a financial planner, to help you design and update your estate plan.

In conclusion, preserving your assets and income is a key aspect of your financial planning. By having enough insurance, a varied investment portfolio, and a thorough estate plan, you may secure your financial stability and well-being from numerous dangers and uncertainties. You should assess your asset and income protection measures often, and make modifications as appropriate, to reflect your changing circumstances and objectives.

Understanding the Impact of Taxes

Taxes are required payments that people and corporations make to the government to finance public goods and services. Taxes may have diverse implications on the economy, society, and the environment, depending on how they are structured and administered. In this article, I will explain some of the primary consequences of taxes on several parts of human existence.

One of the most significant implications of taxes is on the distribution of resources. Taxes may alter the choices and actions of consumers and producers, by changing the relative pricing and incentives of various products and services. For example, a price on tobacco may limit the demand and consumption of smokes, while a subsidy on renewable energy can boost the supply and usage of clean electricity. Taxes may also alter the distribution of income and wealth, by moving money from one group of individuals to another. For example, a progressive income tax may narrow the gap between the affluent and the poor, whereas a regressive sales tax can expand it.

Another influence of taxes is on the efficiency of the economy. Taxes may produce distortions and deadweight losses, by establishing a gap between the private and collective costs and benefits of an activity. For example, a tax on labor may lower the employment and production of the economy, by making people less inclined to work and firms less ready to recruit. Taxes may also cause administrative and compliance expenses, by forcing the government and the taxpayers to spend time and money on collecting and paying taxes. For example, a complicated tax system may raise the paperwork and auditing expenses for both the government and the taxpayers.

A third influence of taxes is on the equality of the society. Taxes may alter the fairness and justice of the tax system, by changing the capacity and desire of various persons to pay taxes. For example, a horizontal equity principle demands that persons with the same income pay the same amount of taxes, whereas a vertical equity principle requires that those with greater income pay more taxes than people with lower income. Taxes may also effect the redistribution and wellbeing of the society, by changing the quantity and quality of public goods and services. For example, a public expenditure principle demands that the benefits of public spending meet the costs of taxes, whereas a benefit principle requires that the consumers of public goods and services pay for them according to their benefits.

In conclusion, taxes may have diverse implications on the economy, society, and the environment, depending on how they are conceived and executed. Taxes may impact the distribution of resources, the efficiency of the economy, and the equality of the society, by altering the prices, incentives, and behaviors of consumers and producers, and by influencing the income, wealth, and welfare of various groups of people. Therefore, knowing the effect of taxes is vital for establishing and assessing a successful tax system that can fulfill the intended aims and objectives of the government and the public.

Chapter 5

Principles of Growing Wealth

PRINCIPLES OF GROWING Wealth

Wealth is the collection of valuable assets that may create income or rise in value over time. Wealth may be quantified in different ways, such as net worth, income, savings, investments, or assets. Growing wealth is the process of growing one's wealth by numerous techniques, such as earning more, saving more, investing better, or spending less. In this post, I will describe some of the ideas of increasing money and how they might be implemented in various scenarios.

Earning More

One of the most apparent methods to create wealth is to earn more money. This may be done by expanding one's talents, education, experience, or network, which can lead to higher-paying employment, promotions, or business possibilities. Earning extra money may also be done by developing several streams of income, such as beginning a side business, freelancing, or creating passive income sources, such as royalties, dividends, or rental income. Earning more money may assist one to save more, invest more, or pay off debts quicker, which can all contribute to creating wealth.

Saving More

Another strategy to increase wealth is to save more money. Saving money is laying away a part of one's salary for future use, such as emergencies, goals, or retirement. Saving money may allow one to avoid debt, cut costs, or amass wealth for investment. Saving money may also assist one to take advantage of compound interest, which is the interest received on interest, which can dramatically enhance one's wealth over time. Saving money may be done by making a budget, monitoring costs, or automating saves, which can allow one to spend less than one earns and save the difference.

Investing Wisely

A third strategy to increase money is to invest properly. Investing money involves putting one's money to work in assets that may create income or grow in value over time, such as stocks, bonds, real estate, or companies. Investing money may allow one to develop one's wealth quicker than saving alone, as one can profit from the power of compounding, diversification, or leverage. Investing money may also allow one to attain financial independence, which is the status of having enough cash to meet one's living needs without working. Investing money may be done by studying the principles of investing, determining a suitable asset allocation, or following a simple and consistent approach, such as index investing, value investing, or dividend investment.

Spending Less

A fourth strategy to increase wealth is to spend less money. Spending money involves utilizing one's money to acquire products or services that can fulfill one's needs or desires. Spending money may help one

Principles of Growing Wealth

Wealth is the amount of valuable resources or assets that one owns. It may be quantified in different ways, including as income, net worth, savings, investments, or quality of life. Wealth may give stability, independence, and opportunity for oneself and others. However, money is not something that is simply obtained or kept. It involves forethought, discipline, and strategy. In this article, I will outline some of the concepts of generating money, based on the study and experience of successful individuals.

Principle 1: Spend Less Than You Earn

The first and most basic premise of generating money is to spend less than you earn. This implies that you have to control your financial flow, and avoid living over your means. Spending less than you earn enables you to save and invest the difference, which may compound over time and build your wealth. To do this, you need to set a budget, manage your spending, and minimize needless costs. You also need to grow your income, by increasing your abilities, obtaining promotions, or establishing various sources of revenue.

Principle 2: Invest Wisely

The second key of creating money is to invest properly. Investing is the act of putting your money to work for you, by purchasing assets that create income or grow in value. Investing may help you develop your money quicker than saving alone, since you can benefit from the power of compounding interest and capital gains. However, investing also carries risk, since you might lose money if the market goes down or the item performs badly. To invest successfully, you need to have a defined aim, a diversified portfolio, a long-term view, and a disciplined approach.

Principle 3: Build Multiple Sources of Income

The third principle of developing wealth is to create diverse sources of income. Having several sources of income suggests that you have more than one method of making money, such as salary, business, dividends, royalties, or rent. Having numerous sources of income may boost your wealth, as you can make more money, minimize your dependency on a single income, and take advantage of diverse possibilities. To establish several streams of income, you need to have an entrepreneurial attitude, a useful talent, a scalable concept, or a passive income strategy.

Principle 4: Leverage Your Time and Money

The fourth element of generating wealth is to leverage your time and money. Leverage is the use of borrowed or other people's resources to increase your own outcomes. Leverage may help you develop your wealth, since you can accomplish more with less, double your income, and generate value for others. To leverage your time and money, you need to have a high return on investment, a strong network, a trusted staff, or a compelling brand.

Principle 5: Learn and Grow Constantly

The fifth and last principle of developing money is to study and progress continually. Learning and developing is the process of learning new information, abilities, and experiences that may boost your personal and professional growth. Learning and developing may help you expand your wealth, since you can adapt to changing situations, solve difficulties, create innovations, and provide value to others. To learn and progress consistently, you need to have an inquisitive mind, a growth mentality, a feedback loop, or a mentor.

In conclusion, gaining money is not a question of luck or accident, but a matter of decision and activity. By following the concepts of spending less than you make, investing intelligently, establishing many sources of income, leveraging your time and money, and learning and improving continually, you may boost your chances of reaching financial success and independence. However, these concepts are not simple to execute, and need dedication, patience, and endurance. Therefore, you should start with little measures, and gradually establish your habits and systems that can help your money building path. Remember, the journey of a thousand miles starts with a single step.

Diversifying Your Portfolio and Sources of Income

Diversification is a technique that seeks to decrease the risk and volatility of an investment portfolio by spreading assets across multiple categories, such as stocks, bonds, commodities, real estate, and cash. Diversification may also refer to having numerous sources of income, such as salary, business, renting, dividend, interest, and royalty. The key advantages of diversity are:

- It decreases the influence of any one asset or income source on the overall performance of the portfolio or the financial status of the person.
- It raises the odds of capturing the returns of diverse asset classes or income streams, which may change based on the market circumstances and economic cycles.
- It offers a buffer against unforeseen occurrences or shocks, such as market collapses, recessions, inflation, currency fluctuations, natural catastrophes, or personal crises.

However, diversity also has its downsides, such as:

- It may diminish the potential return of the portfolio or the person, since certain assets or income sources may have greater predicted returns than others, but also higher risks.
- It may increase the complexity and expense of managing the portfolio or the financial affairs of the person, since additional assets or income streams may involve more research, monitoring, rebalancing, taxes, and fees.
- It may not remove all the risks, since various assets or income streams may be connected or impacted by the same variables, such as global events, systemic hazards, or behavioral biases.

Therefore, diversification should be done with caution and moderation, following certain broad concepts, such as:

- It should be based on the objectives, risk tolerance, time horizon, and particular circumstances of the investor or the individual, rather than on arbitrary rules or figures.

- It should be balanced and diversified across many dimensions, such as asset classes, industries, sectors, geographies, currencies, and income kinds, rather than concentrating on one or a few elements.

- It should be evaluated and updated frequently, since the performance, risk, and correlation of the assets or income sources may vary over time, as well as the requirements and preferences of the investor or the person.

In conclusion, diversity is a beneficial and successful method to strengthen the stability and resilience of an investment portfolio or a financial condition, but it also has certain limits and obstacles. Therefore, it should be executed with care and flexibility, according to the unique aims and circumstances of each investment or person.

Leveraging Passive Income and Compound Interest

Passive income is the revenue that one obtains without active engagement or job, such as from dividends, royalties, rent, or interest. Compound interest is the interest that is computed on the original principle and also on the accumulated interest of prior periods. Both passive income and compound interest may be significant strategies to build one's wealth and financial independence over time, if utilized appropriately.

One of the advantages of passive income is that it may give a stable and continuous stream of income, independent of one's work situation, health, or other conditions. Passive income may also lessen one's dependency on a single income source, and diversify one's portfolio and risk. Moreover, passive income might free up one's time and energy to pursue other objectives, hobbies, or opportunities, such as acquiring new skills, establishing a company, or touring the globe.

One of the drawbacks with passive income is that it generally needs a considerable prior input, either in terms of money, time, or effort. For example, to receive passive income from dividends, one has to acquire shares in a firm that pays dividends consistently. To make passive revenue from royalties, one has to design a product or service that has a large demand and can be sold again. To make passive income from rent, one has to possess a property that can be leased out to renters. To generate passive income from interest, one has to have a big quantity of money or cash that may be loaned out or placed in a bank account.

Another issue with passive income is that it is neither guaranteed or fixed, and may change based on the market circumstances, demand and supply, inflation, taxes, and other things. For example, the dividends of a firm might be lowered or stopped if the company confronts financial problems or losses. The royalties of a product or service might fall or evaporate if the product or service becomes outmoded or loses its appeal. The rent of a property might vary or halt if the property is damaged, unoccupied, or subject to legal challenges. The interest on a loan or deposit might alter or stop if the borrower defaults or the bank collapses.

Therefore, to leverage passive income successfully, one has to have a thorough grasp of the sources, risks, and returns of passive income, and pick the ones that fit one's objectives, preferences, and risk tolerance. One also has to check and manage one's passive income sources periodically, and alter them as required to improve their performance and sustainability.

One of the methods to boost one's passive income is to employ compound interest, which is the interest that is computed on the original principle and also on the accumulated interest of prior periods. Compound interest may exponentially enhance the worth of one's money over time, since the interest is added to the principle and creates additional interest in the following period. For example, if one invests $10,000 at a 10% annual interest rate, compounded yearly, one will get $10,000 x (1 + 0.1) = $11,000 after one year, $11,000 x (1 + 0.1) = $12,100 after two years, and $12,100 x (1 + 0.1) = $13,310 after three years. The entire sum after 10 years will be $25,937.42, which is more than twice the original investment.

One of the elements that determine the potency of compound interest is the frequency of compounding, which is how frequently the interest is computed and added to the principal. The more frequent the compounding, the greater the effective interest rate and the quicker the growth of the money. For example, if one invests $10,000 at a 10% annual interest rate, compounded monthly, one will get $10,000 x (1 + 0.1/12) = $10,083.33 after one month, $10,083.33 x (1 + 0.1/12) = $10,167.14 after two months, and $10,167.14 x (1 + 0.1/12) = $10,251.43 after three months. The total amount after 10 years will be $27,070.41, which is more than the amount with yearly compounding.

Another aspect that influences the potency of compound interest is the time horizon, which is how long one keeps the money invested. The larger the time horizon, the more the compound interest may work its magic and double the money. For example, if one invests $10,000 at a 10% annual interest rate, compounded yearly, one would have $25,937.42 after 10 years, $67,275.00 after 20 years, and $174,494.02 after 30 years. The entire sum after 40 years will be $452,592.56, which is more than 45 times the original investment.

Therefore, to leverage compound interest successfully, one has to start investing as early as possible, pick a high interest rate and a high frequency of compounding, and reinvest the money rather than withdraw it. One also has to be patient and disciplined, and avoid excessive withdrawals, fees, or fines that might lessen the compound interest impact.

In conclusion, passive income and compound interest are two strong instruments that may help one attain financial independence and security over time, if utilized effectively. Passive income may offer a continuous and regular source of income, while compound interest can dramatically enhance the value of one's money. However, both passive income and compound interest need careful planning, administration, and monitoring, as well as a thorough grasp of the sources, risks, and returns involved. By picking the correct passive income sources and employing compound interest to increase them, one may establish a virtuous cycle of wealth generation and accumulation.

Chapter 6

Principles of Sharing Wealth

WEALTH IS THE AMOUNT of valuable resources or material items that one owns or controls. Wealth may be measured in different ways, such as income, assets, net worth, or consumption. Wealth may also be perceived as a source of power, influence, and well-being. However, wealth is not equitably dispersed across persons, communities, or countries. There are enormous disparities and inequities in the distribution of wealth, both within and between nations. These inequities may have detrimental implications on social, economic, and environmental outcomes, such as poverty, health, education, democracy, and sustainability.

Sharing money is the act or practice of sharing or transferring wealth from those who have more to those who have less. Sharing wealth may be done willingly or involuntarily, via numerous means, such as taxes, redistribution, charity, inheritance, or social welfare. Sharing wealth may have diverse purposes, such as alleviating poverty, promoting equality, boosting social cohesion, or supporting progress. Sharing money may also have other impacts, such as enhancing efficiency, encouraging development, improving well-being, or generating tensions.

The principles of sharing money are the moral or ethical criteria that influence or explain the choices and behaviors associated to sharing wealth. These concepts may be acquired from numerous sources, such as philosophy, religion, law, or culture. Different concepts of distributing money may have different assumptions, values, or repercussions. Therefore, there is no one or universal set of rules of distributing wealth that can be applied to all circumstances or settings. However, some viable principles of sharing wealth are:

• The principle of justice: This idea emphasizes that money should be given according to what is fair, right, or merited. This idea might be founded on numerous factors, such as merit, contribution, necessity, or entitlement. For example, this approach may advocate distributing money proportional to how much one has worked, produced, contributed, or endured. This theory may also advocate distributing money according to how much one needs, lacks, or deserves. This philosophy may strive to address or avoid injustices, such as exploitation, oppression, or discrimination, that cause or arise from uneven distribution of income.

• The concept of efficiency: This idea emphasizes that wealth should be dispersed according to what is optimum, helpful, or productive. This approach might be predicated on multiple outcomes, such as utility, welfare, or growth. For example, this theory may encourage distributing money according to how much one can utilize, enjoy, or gain from it. This theory may also encourage distributing money according to how much one can develop, generate, or increase it. This concept may strive to optimize or enhance the overall performance, functioning, or quality of the system, society, or economy that relies on or creates wealth.

• The concept of solidarity: This idea suggests that money should be divided according to what is compassionate, caring, or supporting. This idea might be founded on various ties, such as family, friendship, or community. For example, this approach may encourage distributing money according to how much one is associated, connected, or attached to others. This theory may also advocate distributing money according to how much one is responsible, accountable, or committed to others. This idea may strive to improve or increase the links, ties, or networks that link or unify individuals, communities, or countries that share or rely on money.

These are some of the various principles of sharing money that may be used to guide or assess the choices and behaviors linked to sharing wealth. However, these principles are neither mutually exclusive or comprehensive. They may be merged, adjusted, or augmented by other principles, depending on the unique scenario or setting. Moreover, these principles are not necessarily coherent or congruent. They may clash, contradict, or compete with one other, depending on the diverse viewpoints, interests, or values of the persons, organizations, or countries engaged in sharing wealth. Therefore, distributing wealth is not an easy or clear thing. It is a complicated and demanding topic that demands thoughtful and critical thinking, as well as communication and negotiation, among the numerous stakeholders and players that impact or are affected by sharing wealth.

Giving Back to Society and the Environment

WEALTH IS NOT JUST assessed by the quantity of money or goods one owns, but also by the influence one makes on the world. Wealthy individuals have the ability and the obligation to utilize their wealth for the greater welfare of society and the environment. Giving back is not just a moral requirement, but also a philosophy that may benefit the donor and the recipient in many ways.

One of the advantages of giving back is that it may enhance the quality of life for the less fortunate. By contributing money, commodities, or services to charitable organizations, affluent individuals may assist reduce poverty, hunger, sickness, illiteracy, and other societal ills. They may also support education, health care, arts, culture, and innovation that can better the lives of many people. Giving back may also give possibilities for the impoverished to reach their potential and contribute to society.

Another advantage of giving back is that it may safeguard and repair the environment. By investing in green technology, renewable energy, conservation, and restoration projects, affluent individuals may help cut greenhouse gas emissions, battle climate change, conserve biodiversity, and boost ecosystem services. They may also encourage environmental awareness, education, and activism that can motivate others to take action for the world.

A third advantage of giving back is that it may boost the well-being and pleasure of the donor. By sharing their money, affluent individuals may feel appreciation, pleasure, contentment, and fulfillment. They may also acquire a feeling of purpose, meaning, and connection with others. Giving back may also help their emotional and physical health, as studies have shown that giving can decrease stress, blood pressure, and depression, and boost lifespan and immunity.

In conclusion, giving back to society and the environment is a philosophy of sharing wealth that may have beneficial benefits for the donor, the recipient, and the planet. Wealthy individuals have the ability and the duty to utilize their wealth for the greater good. By doing so, individuals may not only make a difference, but also enhance their own lives.

Planning for Your Legacy and Succession

WHAT IS LEGACY AND succession?

Legacy and succession are two linked ideas that deal with the transmission of money, assets, values, and power from one generation to the next. Legacy is the influence and contribution that a person leaves behind after their death, whereas succession is the process and strategy of passing on leadership, ownership, and control of an organization, company, or family.

Why is preparing for legacy and succession important?

Planning for legacy and succession is crucial for various reasons. First, it may assist maintain and defend the financial stability and well-being of the heirs and beneficiaries, by ensuring that they get their fair portion of the inheritance and prevent excessive taxes, fees, and conflicts. Second, it may assist sustain and increase the reputation and impact of the person or institution that is leaving the legacy, by ensuring that their vision, purpose, values, and objectives are carried on by the successors. Third, it may assist cultivate and promote the social and environmental good that the person or business has done or wants to do, by ensuring that their philanthropic and charitable activities are supported and perpetuated by the successors.

How to prepare for legacy and succession?

Planning for legacy and succession requires various procedures and concerns. Some of the major ones are:

Define your legacy and succession goals and objectives. What do you want to do and accomplish with your legacy and succession? What are your ideals and principles that drive your legacy and succession? Who are your heirs and beneficiaries, and what are their requirements and expectations? How do you wish to be remembered and respected by your successors and the society?

Assess your present status and resources. What are your existing assets and obligations, and how are they dispersed and managed? What are your present sources of income and costs, and how are they influenced by your legacy and succession? What are the legal and fiscal ramifications of your legacy and succession, and how can you minimize them? What are the dangers and obstacles that may effect your legacy and succession, and how can you minimize them?

Design and execute your legacy and succession strategy. How will you pass your riches, possessions, values, and influence to your successors? What are the instruments and methods that you will utilize, such as wills, trusts, insurance, gifts, contributions, etc.? Who are the specialists and consultants that you will contact and work with, such as attorneys, accountants, financial planners, etc.? How will you communicate and coordinate your legacy and succession plan with your successors and stakeholders, such as family members, business partners, workers, customers, etc.?

Review and update your legacy and succession strategy. How frequently will you evaluate and update your legacy and succession strategy, and what are the triggers and signs that will drive you to do so? How will you monitor and assess the development and performance of your legacy and succession strategy, and what are the feedback and evaluation tools that you will use? How will you adapt and change your legacy and succession plan to changing conditions and opportunities, and what are the contingency and backup plans that you will have?

Planning for legacy and succession is a difficult and hard process that demands extensive thinking and planning. However, it is also a gratifying and satisfying activity that may offer peace of mind and happiness to the person or organization that is leaving the legacy, as well as to the successors and beneficiaries who are receiving it. By following the stages and factors indicated above, one may build a legacy and succession plan that matches their beliefs and aims, and that secures their financial, social, and environmental influence and contribution for generations to come.

Summary

The book concepts Governing Wealth and Finance is a thorough guide to understanding and using the underlying concepts that control the production and management of wealth and finance. The book is broken into three parts: Principles of Wealth, Principles of Finance, and Principles of Investing.

Principles of Wealth

The first half of the book explores the notion of wealth and how it may be measured, generated, and dispersed. Wealth is defined as the quantity of products and services that one may purchase with one's money, or the present worth of one's future income. The book highlights four sources of wealth: production, commerce, invention, and inheritance. Production is the process of translating inputs (such as labor, capital, and natural resources) into outputs (such as commodities and services) that have value. Trade is the exchange of commodities and services between people or organizations, which allows for specialization and comparative advantage. Innovation is the production of new or better products and services, or new means of producing or exchanging them, which raise the value of the outputs. Inheritance is the transfer of wealth from one generation to the next, which may be positive (such as gifts, bequests, or contributions) or negative (such as taxes, debts, or obligations).

The book also addresses the elements that impact the production and distribution of wealth, such as productivity, competition, property rights, institutions, culture, demographics, and geography. Productivity is the ratio of outputs to inputs, which defines the efficiency and profitability of production. Competition is the struggle among producers or merchants, which encourages innovation and decreases prices. Property rights are the laws that govern who own something and how they may use it, which offer incentives and security for wealth growth. Institutions are the official and informal norms and institutions that control the conduct of people and groups, which impact the enforcement of property rights, the provision of public goods, and the settlement of disputes. Culture is the collection of values, beliefs, norms, and conventions that determine the choices and behaviors of people and organizations, which impact the motivation and cooperation for wealth development. Demography is the study of the size, structure, and mobility of people, which impact the supply and demand of labor, money, and natural resources. Geography is the physical environment and position of a place, which determine the availability and accessibility of inputs and outputs, as well as the exposure to external shocks and opportunities.

Principles of Finance

The second section of the book explores the notion of finance and how it may be utilized to manage and increase wealth. Finance is described as the science and art of managing money, or the distribution of resources across time and under uncertainty. The book introduces the basic tools and concepts of finance, such as money, interest rates, time value of money, present value, future value, discounting, compounding, cash flows, budgets, financial statements, assets, liabilities, equity, income, expenses, revenues, costs, profits, losses, balance sheet, income statement, cash flow statement, financial ratios, liquidity, solvency, profitability, efficiency, leverage, risk, return, diversification, portfolio, market, price, value, valuation, arbitrage, efficiency, equilibrium, supply, demand, capital, debt, equity, dividends, interest, principal, coupon, maturity, yield, duration, bond, stock, share, dividend, earnings, price-earnings ratio, market capitalization, index, exchange, broker, dealer, bid, ask, spread, order, trade, transaction, commission, fee, tax, regulation, financial market, money market, capital market, primary market, secondary market, spot market, futures market, options market, derivatives market, forex market, commodity market, stock market, bond market, mutual fund, hedge fund, private equity fund, venture capital fund, bank, central bank, commercial bank, investment bank, savings bank, credit union, insurance company, pension fund, endowment fund, foundation, nonprofit organization, corporation, partnership, sole proprietorship, limited liability company, cooperative, financial intermediary, financial institution, financial system, financial sector, financial crisis, financial regulation, financial innovation, financial literacy, financial education, financial planning, financial advice, financial goals, financial strategies, financial decisions, financial behavior, financial psychology, behavioral finance, personal finance, corporate finance, public finance, international finance, and development finance.

The book also discusses the principles and practices of finance, such as saving, investing, borrowing, lending, spending, budgeting, accounting, auditing, reporting, analyzing, forecasting, planning, controlling, managing, financing, funding, raising capital, issuing securities, trading securities, hedging, speculating, arbitraging, pricing, valuing, allocating, diversifying, optimizing, maximizing, minimizing, balancing, matching, netting, discounting, compounding, amortizing, depreciating, appreciating, inflating, deflating, stabilizing, growing, expanding, contracting, merging, acquiring, divesting, restructuring, bankrupting, liquidating, reorganizing, regulating, supervising, monitoring, enforcing, complying, innovating, creating, developing, testing, experimenting, learning, educating, teaching, advising, consulting, coaching, mentoring, guiding, helping, supporting, serving, satisfying, delighting, empowering, enriching, improving, enhancing, benefiting, contributing, adding value, making a difference, making an impact, making a change, making the world a better place, and achieving financial success.

Principles of Investing

The third section of the book explores the notion of investing and how it may be utilized to build and increase wealth. Investing is defined as the act of committing money to an asset or a project with the goal of generating a favorable return in the future. The book defines four sorts of investing: saving, lending, owning, and speculating. Saving is the act of laying away money for future use, such as in a bank account, a certificate of deposit, or a money market fund. Lending is the act of loaning money to a borrower, such as in a bond, a note, or a mortgage. Owning is the act of purchasing a share of ownership in a company or a property, such as in a stock, a real estate, or a private equity. Speculating is the act of speculating on the future price changes of an item or a market, such as in a futures contract, an option, or a derivative.

The book also discusses the factors that affect the performance and risk of investing, such as return, risk, reward, cost, tax, inflation, interest rate, exchange rate, economic growth, business cycle, industry cycle, product cycle, market cycle, market trend, market sentiment, market psychology, market efficiency, market anomaly, market bubble, market crash, market correction, market recovery, market rally, market volatility, market liquidity, market depth, market breadth, market capitalization, market valuation, market diversification, market allocation, market timing, market selection, market strategy, market analysis, market research, market information, market data, market news, market indicator, market signal, market trigger, market catalyst, market event, market factor, market driver, market influencer, market leader, market follower, market laggard, market winner, market loser, market outperformer, market underperformer, market benchmark, market index, market portfolio, market fund, market manager, market advisor, market expert, market guru, market authority, market legend, market icon, market role model, market mentor, market teacher, market learner, market student, **

Don't miss out!

Visit the website below and you can sign up to receive emails whenever MARVEN BILLS publishes a new book. There's no charge and no obligation.

https://books2read.com/r/B-A-YYHDB-IGIVC

BOOKS 2 READ

Connecting independent readers to independent writers.

Also by MARVEN BILLS

The Principles Governing Wealth & Finance

www.ingramcontent.com/pod-product-compliance
Lightning Source LLC
LaVergne TN
LVHW022321200926
848481LV00004B/1392
* 9 7 9 8 2 2 3 0 0 7 2 3 4 *